APA: The Easy Way!

Peggy M. Houghton, Ph.D.
Timothy J. Houghton, Ph.D.
Michael F. Peters, Ph.D.

Editor. Michele M. Pratt

Baker College

Library of Congress Cataloging-in-Publication Data
Houghton, Peggy M.
APA— the easy way! / Peggy M. Houghton, Timothy J. Houghton, Michael F. Peters.
p. cm.
Includes bibliographical references.
ISBN 0-923568-55-7
1. Psychology—Authorship—Handbooks, manuals, etc.
I. Houghton, Timothy J., 1961- II. Peters, Michael F., 1953- III. Title.
BF76.7.H68 2005
808'.06615—dc22
2004026401

Manufactured in the United States of America

Table of Contents

Preface

After 40 combined years of teaching experience, the authors of this handbook have learned that there has been considerable confusion with writing according to the American Psychological Association (APA) guidelines. Those who are familiar with APA format realize that many students arc apprehensive and rather perplexed with this particular writing style.

Although APA writing style is designed for those who intend to publish, numerous colleges and universities adhere to these stringent guidelines. Years of experience have proven that there are consistent questions and misunderstandings regarding the style. Consequently, this document has been developed to make the APA writing experience a much more desirable and simplified learning experience. There are some APA points that are optional; consequently, the instructor should be consulted for final authority with regard to writing assignments.

The intent of this handbook is simply to supplement the official *APA Publication Manual*. It is provided as a condensed version of the actual manual. It is not intended to supersede the manual, rather reduce its complexity. Thus, the title: *APA: The Easy Way!*

The handbook is divided into three parts. Part one focuses on the mechanics of APA format as well as internal text citations; part two emphasizes the actual reference page entries; and part three provides a sample paper.

NOTE: Throughout this document, both single-spacing and boldface type have been utilized. Although this is not in acceptance with the APA writing style, both have been used to simply save space and/or highlight specific rules. In addition, names given throughout are fictitious.

Part One

Mechanics of APA

Utilizing Microsoft Word

The following are specific instructions on how to set up a document for APA format using Microsoft Word.

Margins

All margins (top, bottom, and sides) should be set at one inch. Microsoft Word allows the user to set the margin at a default of one inch. To do so, follow the guidelines below:

1. Under FILE, select PAGE SETUP
2. Select MARGINS tab and type 1" at TOP, BOTTOM, LEFT, and RIGHT boxes

Margins

Alignment/Line Spacing

All documents following APA guidelines are required to be aligned left and double-spaced throughout the entire document. Be sure not to include additional spacing between paragraphs, headings, etc. To set the default, follow these guidelines:

1. Place the cursor at the start of the document, select FORMAT
2. Under FORMAT, select PARAGRAPH
3. Under PARAGRAPH, set ALIGNMENT to LEFT
4. Under PARAGRAPH, set LINE SPACING to DOUBLE

Alignment/ Line spacing

Font Type and Size

The actual font type should be either Times New Roman or Courier. Additionally, APA requires font size to be 12 point.

Font type and size

This is an example of 12-point Times New Roman.
This is an example of 12-point Courier.

To set both the font size and style using Word, do the following:

1. Under FORMAT, select FONT
2. Under FONT, select either Courier or Times New Roman
3. Under SIZE, select 12

Paragraph Indentation

All papers typed in APA format require paragraphs to be indented one-half inch. This can easily be accomplished by striking TAB on the keyboard.

To set tab to the one-half inch default, do the following:

Paragraph indentation

1. Under FORMAT, select PARAGRAPH
2. Under PARAGRAPH, select TABS
3. Under TABS, set DEFAULT TAB STOPS at .5"

Hanging Indents

To set the hanging indent feature, do the following:

Hanging indents

1. Under FORMAT, select PARAGRAPH
2. Under SPECIAL, choose HANGING

> Johnson, L. R. (2001). *People who live in glass houses should not throw stones.* Chicago: Alleman and Anderson Books.

Page Header

Beginning on the very first page of the APA document (title page), a page header should appear. This page header should appear one-half inch down from the top margin and should include the first two or three words of the title of the document, five spaces, and the appropriate page number. Additionally, the page header is right justified. This can be accomplished using the HEADER AND FOOTER function.

Page header

1. Under VIEW, select HEADER AND FOOTER
2. Select the page number icon (the first icon on left with the # symbol); the number will appear on the left side of the

box. The cursor will appear to the right of the number. Move the cursor, using the left arrow key, to the left of the number. Press the spacebar five times, thus moving the number correspondingly. Move the cursor to the left margin. At this point, type the first two to three words of the title.

3. Highlight the entire typed portion, including both the title and the number

4. Hit the align right key located in the toolbar

Page header

In-text Citations

General Comments

- Do not use boldface type with APA format

- Use third-person only with APA format

- Person refers to the writer's viewpoint. First-person is the writer speaking; second-person is the person being spoken to; and third-person is the person being spoken about

- First-person pronouns include the following: I, me, my, mine (singular); we, us, our, ours (plural)

- Second-person pronouns include the following: you, your, yours (singular and plural)

In-text citations

- Third-person pronouns include the following: he, she, it, him, her, his, hers (singular); they, them, their, theirs (plural)

- The first line of every paragraph (other than the abstract) should be indented five spaces. Again, if the TAB key defaults at .5, simply strike the TAB key

- Always provide appropriate credit; otherwise, it is considered plagiarism

- Everything cited in the text must appear in the Reference page; likewise, everything cited in the Reference page must appear within the text

In-text citations

- When paraphrasing an author, the punctuation (period) should be placed after the actual reference citation. For example:

> (Robbins, 2004).

Not

> .(Robbins, 2004)

- When citing a direct quotation less than 40 words, the punctuation (period) should be placed after the actual reference citation. For example:

> (Smith, 2001, p. 6).

Not

> .(Smith, 2001, p. 6)

- When citing a direct quotation 40 words or greater, the entire quotation is indented and no quotation marks are required. The indentation implies that it is a direct quote. For example:

> In their book *Between a Rock and a Hard Place* (1993), Roueche and Roueche include a memorable quote from a developmental writing teacher just completing the first year of teaching in a downtown community college.
>
> > I find it amazing that so many of my students will work so hard to make it when there is so little in their past to give them the confidence to try; I also find it remarkable that they finally achieve so much in spite of what at first appears to be overwhelming academic and personal odds; but what I find most unbelievable is that they take the chance and even come at all. (Roueche & Roueche, 1993, p. 121)

NOTE: When citing a direct quotation that is 40 words or greater, the punctuation (period) is placed before the actual reference citation.

- Use a variety of writing style techniques. Do not end every paragraph with the standard method of citing (author's last name, date published). This flexibility will allow for a more logical flow of reading. For example, use different techniques such as the following:

| According to Stemmer (2004)… |

or

| Stemmer (2004) indicated… |

In-text citations

Levels of Headings

When a document requires the use of headings, the following five levels should be utilized (*Publication Manual of the American Psychological Association*, 2001, pp. 113-115):

CENTERED UPPERCASE HEADING (Level 5)

Centered Uppercase and Lowercase Heading (Level 1)

Centered, Italicized, Uppercase and Lowercase Heading (Level 2)

Flush Left, Italicized, Uppercase and Lowercase Side Heading (Level 3)

    Indented, italicized, lowercase heading ending with a period; paragraph begins on same line (Level 4)

NOTE: In level four headings, capitalize only the first letter of the first word.

One level: For a short article, one level heading may be sufficient. In such cases, use only centered uppercase and lowercase headings (Level 1).

Levels of headings

Two levels: For many articles in APA journals, two levels of heading meet the requirements. Use Level 1 and Level 3 headings.

Three levels: For many articles, three levels of heading are needed. Use Level 1, Level 3, and Level 4 headings.

Levels of headings

Four levels: For some articles, particularly multiexperiment studies, monographs, and lengthy literature reviews, four levels of heading are needed. Use heading Levels 1 through 4.

Five levels: Occasionally, an article requires five levels of heading. In such cases, subordinate all four levels above by introducing a Level 5 heading – a centered uppercase heading – above the other four.

Title Page

The title page of the document should include the following:

Title page

- Running head (upper left-hand corner – one inch from top)
- Page header (upper right-hand corner – one half inch from top)
- Title of the paper, student's name, and name of college or university centered on the page

The Running head will appear one inch from the top of the page. The R is uppercase, while the h is lowercase. After the words Running head, there is a colon, two spaces, and the title of the paper typed in all caps. Note that this is the only part of the APA document that will appear in all uppercase lettering. Also, there is a limit of 50 maximum total characters starting after the colon...counting spaces. It may be necessary to use only main words of the title.

Running head: MOTIVATING EMPLOYEES

The page header will appear one-half inch from the top margin. The first two or three words of the paper, followed by five spaces, and the appropriate page number should be included. The page header should start on the title page and run consistently through-out the entire document. The header feature in Word should be utilized when establishing the page header (see page 2).

The title of the paper, student's name, and name of college or university should be typed in that order and be centered on the title page (see Part Three for example).

Abstract

The word Abstract should be centered, one inch from the top of the page. The actual abstract, however, should be left justified. This is the only paragraph of the paper that is not indented. It should be **Abstract** concise, accurate, and reflect the content of the document. The abstract should be only one paragraph in length and not exceed 120 words. No paraphrasing or direct quotes should be included (see Part Three for example).

Table of Contents

The table of contents is optional with the 5th edition APA manual; **Table of** it is not one of the required elements of the writing style. Instruc- **contents** tors may or may not wish to include this as a requirement. It is at the discretion of the individual instructor.

Appendices

Appendices are pages at the end of the paper (after the references) with additional information. Appendices allow the author to in- **Appendices** clude information that would be distracting to the reader if included in the body of the paper. Tables or charts more than a half page in length are often placed in the appendices rather than the text of the paper.

Body of Paper

Writers are strongly encouraged to develop the Reference page prior to in-text citations. This simplifies the process of writing the in-text citations, as these citations are derived from the actual reference page.

Consistent errors generally occur throughout citing in the text of the document. Although there is no specific order regarding the APA rules, the bulleted points below appear to be the most common errors found in student papers.

Para-phrasing

• *Paraphrasing an author*

When paraphrasing one author, provide the author's last name and the publication year. Note that the author's name and year are separated by a comma.

(Tisdelle, 2004).

Note that the actual punctuation (period) is placed only after the citation…not before or before and after.

• *Order of multiple authors*

When using a source with more than one author, always list the authors in the same order listed in the book or article.

Multiple authors

• *Direct quotes*

There are two different types of direct quotes.

When stating a direct quote (verbatim) that is less than 40 words, the entire quotation is placed in quotation marks. The actual reference citation should include the author's last name, the year published, and the page number where the quote can be located.

Direct quotes

There are a few things to consider at this point. The end quotation mark should appear at the end of the last word in the quote. However, the punctuation (at the end of the quote) is placed after the actual citation. In addition, the abbreviation for page is p. If using multiple pages, the abbreviation is pp.

(Heberling & Houghton, 2005, pp. 8-9).

Not

. (Heberling & Houghton, 2005, pp. 8-9)

When citing a direct quote that is 40 words or greater, the entire quotation is indented and no quotation marks are required, as the indentation implies that it is a direct quote. In this particular case, **Direct** the punctuation (period) is placed before the actual citation, not **quotes** after.

.(Houghton et al., 2005, p. 8)

Also, when a quotation that is 40 words or greater has a second paragraph, the second paragraph of the blocked quotation is indented.

In their book titled, *Modern Day CEOs the Good the Bad and the Ugly* (2002), Heberling and Houghton noted the following:

Throughout her troubled youth, Oprah would always have a refuge. She would turn to books as a safe haven. She was, and still is, an avid reader. Reading gave her hope and gave her the will to aspire to new goals. Oprah was exceptionally intelligent. Her strong intellect allowed her to skip both kindergarten and second grade. Oprah always praised her teachers for their guidance and support throughout her early years.

Although Oprah lived with a myriad of people throughout her lifetime, she credits her grandmother for making her the success that she is today. This is primarily because her grandmother acted as the dominant support figure during her youth. It was her grandmother, and later her father, who were the ones who expected the best out of her; they expected her to excel with everything she did. Time would prove this to be an expectation that was ultimately conquered. (p. 196)

- *Secondary Sources*

When citing a source within a source, name the original work and give a citation for the secondary source. For example, if citing a paraphrased comment from Stemmer in Pratt's article (when Stemmer's original work was not read), reference the citation as follows:

Secondary sources

(Stemmer, as cited in Pratt, 2004)

NOTE: If a direct quote was stated from Stemmer, the page number must also be included. Also, only Pratt's work is cited on the reference page.

Author, Date Reference Citations

One author:

Citing one author

When paraphrasing one author, provide the author's last name and the publication year. Note that the author's name and year are separated by a comma.

(Karsten, 2004).

Two authors:

Citing two authors

When citing two authors, use both authors' names every time and the symbol & when used inside parentheses.

(Heberling & Houghton, 2002).

Three, four, or five authors:

Citing multiple authors

When citing three, four, or five authors, cite all authors in the first reference citation; in subsequent citations, use only the last name of the first author followed by the Latin term et al. For example (using the authors of this handbook):

[*first citation*]: (Houghton, Houghton, & Peters, 2005)

[*subsequent citations*]: (Houghton et al., 2005).

Note that there is a period only after al.

Six or more authors:

When citing work from six or more authors, always use only

the last name of the first author followed by et al. For example, when citing work from Curtis, Jones, Brown, Johnson, Workman, and Smith, use the following:

Citing multiple authors

> (Curtis et al., 2004)

No author listed:
When citing work with no author, the first few words of the actual reference page entry should be used. Titles of books should be italicized, while chapters or articles should be noted in double quotation marks.

No author listed

> Some individuals believe that leadership is an innate skill that simply cannot be learned (*The mystery of leadership*, 2004)
>
> Leadership is not a scientific art ("Leadership versus management," 2004)

Anonymous author:
When citing work where the author is listed as Anonymous, cite the term Anonymous.

Anonymous author

> (Anonymous, 2004)

Authors with the same last name:
When using different authors with the same last name, use the first name initial within the text citation.

Authors with the same last name

> T. Houghton (2005) and P. Houghton (2002) extensively discuss leadership characteristics in Fortune 500 companies.

Multiple articles from the same author:
When citing the same author with more than one publication within the same year, list the dates including a, b, c, etc. See page 17 for a Reference page example.

Multiple articles from the same author

> Several published documents by Presnal (2004a, 2004b, 2004c, and 2004d)…

Personal communication:

When citing personal interviews, personal correspondence, or e-mail communications, state the interviewee's name followed by parentheses noting personal communication and the date which the communication occurred.

> Talking with Macklin (personal communication, May 30, 2004)...

Personal communi- cation

- Since this cannot be verified, no reference page entry is necessary.
- In subsequent in-text citations, use the last name and year of interview.

Electronic references:

When no page number is provided with electronic sources, cite the paragraph number when possible. This can be accomplished by using either the paragraph symbol (¶) or the paragraph abbreviation (para.). In situations where the paragraph numbers are not provided, give the subtitle of the section along with the number of the paragraph within the section.

Electronic references

> (McDowell, 2004, para. 2)
> (McDowell, 2004, Union Power section, para. 2)

NOTE: All electronic references are cited in the same format as other citations. In other words, when paraphrasing, simply use the author's name and year published. If no author is provided, use the first few words of the title (italicized) and year published. When completed in this format, the reader can reference the actual reference page to get the specific web page address and other citation information.

E-mail references:

> According to Paul Carey (personal communication, October 6, 2004), radio broadcasting is a challenging yet very rewarding career.

E-mail references

- Again, since e-mail communication cannot always be retrieved, no reference page entry is required.

Part Two

Reference Page

A list of references should be given on a separate page(s) at the end of an APA document. Every reference cited in the text should be listed in the reference page(s), and every reference listed in the reference page(s) should be cited in the text. However, note that secondary sources are not necessary as an entry in the reference page...only the original source.

References are a critical aspect of a paper since they allow readers to find and utilize sources cited in the text. References also indicate the vigilance of the writer, so a concerted effort should be made to pay attention to details (proper spelling, accurate information, punctuation, etc.). Most importantly, the reference section provides proper credit to authors for their work, which is why all information listed should be accurate and complete.

General 5th edition APA guidelines for the reference page(s) include:

In General

- Margins should be one inch all around (top, bottom, left and right)
- The page heading should be centered and called References
- Double spacing should be used (examples used in this section are single spaced in order to save space)

Format

- Bold type should not be used
- Underlining should not be used in the reference page
- Professional credentials should be used in the reference page (i.e. Ph.D.)
- Personal conversations, e-mails, interviews, and letters should not be listed since the reader is unable to retrieve these types of sources (cite as personal communication in text, but do not list in the reference page)
- The first line of each reference entry should start at the left margin with the following lines being indented approximately one half inch (hanging indent)
- References beginning with numerals should have the numeral spelled out

Numerals

"3 times the fun: The joy of triplets" should be listed as "Three times the fun: The joy of triplets"

- Acceptable abbreviations include:

ed.	Edition
2nd ed.	Second Edition
Ed.	Editor
Eds.	Editors
Rev. ed.	Revised Edition
Vol.	Volume (as in Vol. 1)
Vols.	Volumes (as in 3 Vols.)
p.	Page
pp.	Pages
No.	Number
Pt.	Part
n.d.	No Date
chap.	Chapter
Tech. Rep.	Technical Report
Suppl.	Supplement

Abbreviations

- States should use two letter abbreviations

AK	Alaska
MI	Michigan
WV	West Virginia

- References should be listed in alphabetical order by authors (using surname of first author), associations (if the author is unknown, but not anonymous), and Anonymous (if work is signed Anonymous). Authors should be listed with last name first, followed by first and middle (if given) initials. If no author is provided, the entry should be alphabetized according to the first word of the title (except a, an, the).

When listing by author(s)

- First and middle initials only should be used (no complete first or middle names)

> Comos, M. E. (2002) should be used for a 2002 article authored by Michael Eugene Comos

- For one author, list author before date

> Schreck, E. P. (2003). *Mistakes of supervising a culturally diverse workforce in the USDA*. Boston: Corrigan Books.

- For two to six authors, separate authors with commas and use an ampersand (&) before the last author's name, followed by the date

> Sienkiewicz, J. H., Scarcelli, T. A., & Alexandrowicz, M. P. (2002). *Great high school athletes transition into coaching roles*. Clawson, MI: Roddy Press.

- For seven or more authors, separate the first six authors with commas, then use et al. for the remaining authors, followed by the date

> Partz, M., Mentro, J. P., Harcelli, T., Banshi, P. P., Cretzell, G., Smith, C. E., et al. (2003). A qualitative study of modern Native American dance. *Journal of Dance Methodology, 12*(3), 12-21.

Multiple authors

- The publication date should be placed in parentheses after the author's name(s)

> Harcourt, J. (2004). The influence of peer pressure on dating within the same group of friends. *Journal of Social Interaction, 55*(6), 312-319.

NOTE: The entire date should be used when citing a magazine article. In journal articles, it is necessary to use only the year, assuming that the issue number is provided.

- Use (n.d.) after the author's name if no date is available

> Zajciw, P. (n.d.). *Ukrainian culture in United States' elementary schools*. Miami, FL: Dolson Books.

- Use (in press) after the author's name if his or her work is in press (not yet published)

Publication dates

> Bojelay, M. J. (in press). *Beginning a successful career in real estate: Ten secrets you need to know.* Chicago: Petersville.

- List publication dates chronologically (the earliest first) if an author has more than one reference entry cited

> Ahern, J. (2001). *The beginning of electricity*. New York: Lawrence House.
>
> Ahern, J. (2002). *Electricity as we know it today*. New York: Lawrence House.
>
> Ahern, J. (2004). *Electricity in the future*. New York: Lawrence House.

- Multiple citations containing the same author should list the individual author first (regardless of date)

Talbot, B. P. (2001). *Marketing retail cosmetics in California.* New York: Mitch Clawson Press.

Talbot, B. P., & Peace, J. (2000). *Packaging technology in the United Kingdom.* New York: Mitch Clawson Press.

- Multiple citations containing the same author and year should be listed alphabetically by the title of the book or article. A lowercase a, b, c etc. should be used after the year to distinguish the entries. This is also used in the in-text citations.

Munson, R. (2002a). *Human socialization at home.* Chicago: Hawthorne Press.

Munson, R. (2002b). *Human socialization at work.* Chicago: Hawthorne Press.

Multiple citations by the same author

- Multiple citations containing the same author and different second or third authors should be listed alphabetically by the surname of the second author (or third author if the second author is the same)

Jones, T., & Henson, R. I. (2002). *Fire prevention in schools.* Philadelphia: Johannesburg Books.

Jones, T., & Timocco, M. (2001). *Fire prevention at work.* Philadelphia: Johannesburg Books.

Jones, T., Timocco, M., & Smith, R. L. (2003). *Fire prevention at home.* Philadelphia: Johannesburg Books.

Jones, T., Timocco, M., & Yandley, P. T. (1999*). Fire: A historical analysis.* Philadelphia: Johannesburg Books.

When listing by association (if author is unknown, but not anonymous)

• The association should use upper and lowercase letters

> American Psychological Association
>
> The Florida Guide to College Scholarships

Entries by association

• The publication date should be placed in parentheses after the association

> Patrick S. Houghton Heart Foundation. (2001).

• Use (n.d.) after the association if no date is available

> Warren Woods High School. (n.d.).

• Use (in press) after the association if the work is in press (not yet published)

> *Detroit Cancer Society Membership Directory.* (in press).

Anonymous author

When listing by Anonymous (if signed Anonymous)

• The word Anonymous should be used if the work is signed Anonymous (alphabetize this as if Anonymous is a true name)

> Anonymous. (2003).

When listing publishers

• Full names should be used for any university press or association acting as publisher

> Wayne State University Press

Publisher entries

• Unessential terms such as Co. or Publishers should be excluded, but terms such as Press or Books should be included

Johnson Co. should be listed as Johnson

Herndén Books should be listed as Herndén Books

• The city and state should be listed for United States publishers in cities not known for publishing (use United
States Postal Service two letter abbreviations for states)

**Publisher
entries**

Springfield, IL: Herndén Books

Fort Wayne, IN: Preston

• The city only (no state) may be listed for U. S. cities that
are major publishing centers

Baltimore	Boston
Chicago	Los Angeles
New York	Philadelphia
San Francisco	

• The city, state, province, and country should be listed
for non-United States publishers in cities not known for
publishing

Windsor, Ontario, Canada: Thompson Books

Berlin, Germany: Mueller

• The city only may be listed for non-United States cities
that are major publishing centers

Amsterdam: Goelic	Milan: Bobsoni
Jerusalem: Islala Books	Rome: Santo
Moscow: Dosky	Paris: Frolee Books
Stockholm: Beckwoth	Tokyo: Tei Wei
Vienna: Ser Gut	
London: Fenton University Press	

- The state should not be repeated if it is included in the publishing name

> The Ohio State University Press: Columbus

When listing page numbers

- The abbreviation p. (one page) or pp. (multiple pages) should be used for newspapers. These abbreviations should be used in book citations only when referencing a chapter or a section of a book.

> p. C1 should be used instead of C1 for a newspaper reference
>
> p. 21 should be used for one page in a book
>
> pp. 312-321 should be used for multiple pages in a book

Page numbers

- Periodicals other than newspapers should use page numbers only

> Johnson, R. (2000). Talk on the streets. *American Psychological Review, 87*(3), 521-529.

- All numbers (figures) should be listed for inclusive page numbers

> 521-529 should be used instead of 521-9

Books

- In general, a book reference should list the author(s), publication date, title, edition [if other than first], and publishing information

> Jackson, L. P. (2004). *The times are changing for urban developers* (2nd ed.). Boston: Allester and Bacon.

- A book title should be italicized, and only the first letter and proper nouns should be capitalized (unless using a colon, period, question mark, or exclamation point; then

the first letter after the punctuation should also be capitalized)

> *Modern management gurus*
>
> *Racism in the workplace: The war wages on*
>
> *Forget the stress. Start living better today*
>
> *Never give in without a fight! The basics of negotiation*

- A book with no author or editor should list the title, the
  year, and then the publishing information

Book entries

> *Communication in the workplace.* (2001). Cambridge,
>   NJ: Boston Books.

- An edited book should list (Ed.) or (Eds.) after the editor(s)
  names

> Dewa, P., & Runkel, G. (Eds.). (2002). *Chess strategies
>   made simple.* New York: Davidson Books.

- A revised edition of a book should list (Rev. ed.) after the
  title

> Williams, D. (2004). *Physical therapy and the aging athlete*
>   (Rev. ed.). Detroit, MI: Wayne State University Press.

- A subsequent edition of a book should list the edition in
  parentheses after the title

> Lapensee, D. L. (in press). *Financial incentives behind
>   sibling rivalries in family business* (2nd ed.). Baltimore:
>   BBM College Press.

- A book published by the author should list Author as the
  publisher

> American Psychological Association. (2001). *Publication
>   manual of the American Psychological Association*
>   (5th ed.). Washington, DC: Author.

- A chapter in an edited book should list the author(s), publication date of book, chapter title, book editor(s), book title, pages, and publishing information

> Shurlez, S. S. (2003). Rethinking manufacturing. In P. J. Samakal (Ed.), *Modern business strategies* (pp. 63-78). New York: Pemberton Books.

- An article in an edited book should list the author(s), publication date of book, article title, book editor(s), book title, pages, and publishing information

> Czajowski, A. (2002). Asian politics. In P. T. Homes (Ed.), *World politics today* (pp. 87-99). Chicago: Wiley Books.

Articles within books

- An article in a volume in a series should list the author(s), publication date of book, article title, series editor, volume editor, volume title, volume number, volume series, edition, pages, and publishing information

> Cook, T. C. (2001). Meat inspection in pilot plants. In D. K. Wlasiuk (Series Ed.) & J. K. Grems (Vol. Ed.), *Meat Inspection:* Vol. 4. *Small plant issues* (4th ed., pp. 27-34). Los Angeles: Hillman.

- An encyclopedia or dictionary should list the author(s) [if signed], publication date, subject title (if available), editor(s) (if given), book title, edition, volume(s), page(s), and publishing information

> Ritter, J. R., & Wells, P. (2003). Physical strength. In J. R. Ritter, & P. Wells, *The British encyclopedia* (4th ed.). London: Avonhurst Books.
>
> Mackson, P. D., & Erickson, T. I. (Eds.). (2001). *Johnson's dictionary of psychiatry* (5th ed., Vols. 1-19). New York: Massillon.

> Peters, V., & Henz, T. R. (2003). Fossil fuel. In *The new world encyclopedia* (Vol. 19, pp. 440-449). Boston: New World Encyclopedia.

- An encyclopedia with no author or editor should list the subject title, publication date, book title, edition (if given), volume, pages, and publishing information

> Missouri. (2004). In *The encyclopedia of the Americas* (Vol. 21, pp. 210-218). Dripping Springs, TX: Encyclopedia of the Americas.

Encyclopedias and dictionaries

- A dictionary with no author or editor should list the book title, edition (if given), publication date, and publishing information

> *Merriam-Webster's collegiate dictionary* (12th ed.). (2003). Springfield, MA: Merriam-Webster.

- A manual published by an association should list the association, year, book title, edition (if given), and publishing information

> American Dental Association. (2003). *Diagnostic manual of gum disease* (6th ed.). Fort Wayne, IN: Author.

- A multi-volume edited reference published over multiple years should list the editor(s), publication date, book title, volumes, pages, and publishing information

> Buckholder, T., & Schnelling, P. R. (Eds.) (1998). *Multiple sclerosis: A history in England* (Vol. 1, pp. 68-84). London: Wells University Press.

Brochures

- In general, a brochure reference should list the author (or organization), publication date, brochure title [Brochure], and publishing information

> Hartville Symphony. (2004). *Enjoy the music of Jim "the candyman" Smith* [Brochure]. Hartville, OH: Baynes University Press.

Brochures

- A brochure title should be italicized, and only the first letter and proper nouns should be capitalized (unless using a colon, period, question mark, or exclamation point; then the first letter after the punctuation should also be capitalized)

> *The George Washington educational center tour*

- A brochure published by the author should list Author as the publisher

> Ohio Meat and Poultry Institute. (2003). *Guidelines for reducing pathogenic bacteria in poultry* [Brochure]. North Canton, OH: Author.

Newsletters

- In general, a newsletter reference should list the author(s), publication date, article title, title of newsletter [Newsletter], volume, issue, and pages

> Richards, K. (2004, July). Reinhardt Avenue to be repaved this fall. *Town Acres* [Newsletter]*, 7*(3), 2-3.

News-letters

NOTE: Only list numbers…do not use p. or pp.

NOTE: The volume and issue number are required for newsletters. In the previous example, 7 = volume number while 3= issue number. The volume number is italicized. The issue number is placed in parentheses, with no space or punctuation between the volume and issue.

- Newsletter titles should be italicized, using upper and lowercase letters (significant words should be capitalized)

> *Harlwood Herald*

- An article title should not be italicized or placed in quotation marks, and only the first letter and proper nouns should be capitalized (unless using a colon, period, question mark, or exclamation point, then the first letter after the punctuation should also be capitalized)

> Food drive to be held in church parking lot

Journals

- An article title should not be italicized or placed in quotation marks, and only the first letter and proper nouns should be capitalized (unless using a colon, period, question mark, or exclamation point; then the first letter after the punctuation should also be capitalized)

> Do employees really love their jobs? Studies indicate 'yes.'

- In general, a journal reference should list the author(s), publication date, article title, journal title, volume, issue, and pages

> Roddy, P. K (2000). A study of communication between a 1964 rock band and youth: The influence of The Rolling Stones on American teenagers. *Journal of Social Commentary, 23*(2), 254-287.

NOTE: Only list numbers...do not use p. or pp.

NOTE: The volume and issue number are required for journals. In the previous example, 23 = volume number while 2 = issue number. The volume number is italicized. The issue number is placed in parentheses, with no space or punctuation between the volume and issue.

- A journal supplement should list the author(s), publication date, article title, journal title, volume, supplement, and pages

> Bush, C. T. (2002). Coping with difficult jobs: First level management revelations. *Research Technology Management, 35* (Suppl. 2), 11-13.

- Journal titles should be italicized, using upper and lowercase letters (significant words should be capitalized)

> *Journal of Applied Physics*

Magazines

- In general, a magazine reference should list the author(s), entire publication date, article title, magazine title, volume, and pages

> Hoban, D. M. (2003, July 23). Fighting high cholesterol in diabetic adults. *Healthweek 12*(2), 54-57.

NOTE: Only list numbers...do not use p. or pp.

NOTE: The volume number is required for magazines. In the previous example, 12 = volume number while 2 = issue number (optional). The volume number is italicized. The issue number, if used, is placed in parentheses, with no space or punctuation between the volume and issue.

Magazines

- Magazine titles should be italicized, using upper and lowercase letters (significant words should be capitalized)

> *Modern Investing*

- An article title should not be italicized or placed in quotation marks, and only the first letter and proper nouns should be capitalized (unless using a colon, period, question mark, or exclamation point; then the first letter after the punctuation should also be capitalized)

> The market crash: Are we done yet?

Newspapers

- In general, a newspaper reference should list the author(s), entire publication date, article title, newspaper title, and pages (separate pages with a comma)

> Helm, T. R. (2003, May 23). Terrorism in the food chain. *The Montgomery Times*, pp. A1, A11.

NOTE: Use p or pp. before page numbers.

- An article with no author should list the article title, publication date, newspaper title, and pages (separated by commas)

> Gambling: Who really loses? (2002, January 27). *The Shreveport Gazette*, pp. B5, B12.

- A letter to the editor should list [Letter to the editor] after the title

> Yastremski, P. R. (2004, August 21). Olympics need stricter drug screening protocol [Letter to the editor]. *The Alabama Daily*, p. C2.

- Newspaper titles should be italicized, using upper and lowercase letters (significant words should be capitalized)

> *The Cincinnati Tribune*

- An article title should not be italicized or placed in quotation marks, and only the first letter and proper nouns should be capitalized (unless using a colon, period, question mark, or exclamation point; then the first letter after the punctuation should also be capitalized)

> Simpson wins primary by a landslide!

Reports

- In general, a report reference should list the author (or organization), publication date, report title, issue number (or report number), and publishing information

> United States Mental Health Service. (2004). *Statistical data for psychological research* (USMHS Publication No. 43). Washington, DC: U.S. Government Printing Office.

- A university report should list the name of the reporting department after the university name

> Kowlakowski, D., & Martz, D. (2003). *Eliminating mercury in fillings* (Report to the dean). Minneapolis, MN: Delta University Press, Dental Committee.

Reports

- A report published by the author should list Author as the publisher

> Harlem Music Institute. (2003). *Hip-hop in urban areas* (HMI Report No. 12). New York: Author.

- A report from the National Technical Information Service (NTIS) or the Educational Resources Information Center (ERIC) should list the author (or organization), publication date, title, report number, publishing information, and ERIC or NTIS number

> Melloni, T. J., & Weller, P. (2003). *The health risks of asbestos in old homes* (Report No. SCRLL-TT-92-3). East Lansing, MI: National Center for Cancer Research. (ERIC Document Reproduction Service No. SC1120998)

- A report title should be italicized, and only the first letter and proper nouns should be capitalized (unless using a colon, period, question mark, or exclamation point; then the first letter after the punctuation should also be capitalized)

> *Safety research comparisons for the Ford compact vehicles*

Published Contribution to a Meeting

- In general, a published contribution to a meeting should list the author(s), publication date, title of published contribution, meeting, pages, and publishing information

> Randazzo, T., & Somerset, D. (2003). Progress in the development of an anti-microbial agent for inhibiting pathogenic bacteria. In *Midwestern Status Symposium of Meat Processors* (pp. 12-17). Dayton, OH: University of Dayton Press.

- A published contribution to a meeting with no author should list the title, publication date, meeting, pages, and publishing information

Meeting presentations

> Ronald Reagan: Great communicator or great manipulator? (2001). In *The Political Century Symposium* (pp. 217-229). White Plains, NY: Orson College Press.

- A published contribution title presented at a meeting should be italicized, and only the first letter and proper nouns should be capitalized (unless using a colon, period, question mark, or exclamation point, then the first letter after the punctuation should also be capitalized)

> *Archeological findings in northern Japan*

Reviews

- In general, a review for a motion picture, video, or book should list the author(s), date, title [the medium being reviewed], the source containing the review, volume, issue, and pages

Hemp, J. P. (2004). The reality of religion [Review of the motion picture *The passion*]. *Visual Psychology, 51*(1), 312-317.

Marly, T. (2004). Fact or fiction [Review of the book *My life*]. *Basic Science, 27(3)*, 210-213.

Partley, B., & Bobson, T. R. (2004). Why the fuss [Review of the video *Straight talk*]. *Video Review, 21*(2), 21-44.

Reviews

- A review for a motion picture, video, or book should have the title (of that being reviewed) italicized, and only the first letter and proper nouns should be capitalized (unless using a colon, period, question mark, or exclamation point; then the first letter after the punctuation should also be capitalized)

Understanding emotional intelligence

- The source containing the review should be italicized, using upper and lowercase letters (significant words should be capitalized)

Contemporary Psychology

Dissertations and Theses

- In general, a doctoral dissertation obtained in DAI (Dissertation Abstracts International) from UMI should list the author, publication date, title, Dissertation Abstracts International, DAI volume, DAI issue, page(s), and UMI number

Carthworth, J. A. (2003). The portrayal of young African American females in hip-hop music video. *Dissertation Abstracts International, 51*(03), 541B. (UMI No. 8014327)

- Dissertation Abstracts International should be italicized, using upper and lowercase letters

Dissertation Abstracts International

- A doctoral dissertation title obtained from UMI should not be italicized or placed in quotation marks, and only the first letter and proper nouns should be capitalized (unless using a colon, period, question mark, or exclamation point; then the first letter after the punctuation should also be capitalized)

A statistical analysis of Hispanic females earning advanced college degrees

- A doctoral dissertation obtained in DAI from a university should list the author, publication date, title, Doctoral dissertation, university, publication date, Dissertation Abstracts International, DAI volume, DAI issue, and page(s)

Riles, P. M. (2002). An analysis of war: Looking back at Viet Nam (Doctoral dissertation, University of Kentucky, 2002). *Dissertation International Abstracts, 49(01),* 226.

- An unpublished doctoral dissertation should list the author, publication date, title, Unpublished doctoral dissertation, and university

Billesti, M. R. (2004). The effects of aging on Asian population growth. Unpublished doctoral dissertation, University of Michigan, Ann Arbor.

- In general, a published Master's thesis obtained in Master Abstracts International from a university should list the author, publication date, title, Master's thesis, university, publication date, Masters Abstracts International, volume, and pages

Dissertations and theses

Chudzik, S. (2003). A study in motivation of production employees: Applying Locke's goal setting theory (Master's thesis, Warsaw University, 2003). *Masters Abstracts International, 52*, 61.

Dissertations and theses

- Masters Abstracts International should be italicized, using upper and lowercase letters

Masters Abstracts International

- A master's thesis title obtained in Masters Abstract International should not be italicized or placed in quotation marks, and only the first letter and proper nouns should be capitalized (unless using a colon, period, question mark, or exclamation point; then the first letter after the punctuation should also be capitalized)

Researching the impact of the World Series: A qualitative analysis

Unpublished Works from a University

Unpublished works

- An unpublished manuscript title from a university should be italicized, and only the first letter and proper nouns should be capitalized (unless using a colon, period, question mark, or exclamation point; then the first letter after the punctuation should also be capitalized)

The decline of liberalism in America

- An unpublished manuscript from a university should list the city and state (if not part of the university name)

Flint, MI: Baker College

East Lansing: Michigan State University

Electronic Media (non-Internet)

Motion Picture

- In general, a motion picture should list the names of major contributors with their titles in parentheses, publication date, title [Motion picture], country, and studio

Roots, K. (Producer), & Dumars, J. (Director). (2004). *On the road with an NBA championship team* [Motion picture]. United States: Waver Pictures.

Motion pictures

- A motion picture title should be italicized, and only the first letter and proper nouns should be capitalized (unless using a colon, period, question mark, or exclamation point; then the first letter after the punctuation should also be capitalized)

On golden pond

- A motion picture should list the country where the picture was made and the name of the studio

United States: United Artists

Television

- In general, a television broadcast should list the producer, publication date, title [Television broadcast], city, state, and station

Television

Belechik, G. (Producer). (2003, September 1). *Scared to speak out* [Television broadcast]. New York: WMTW.

- A television broadcast title should be italicized, and only the first letter and proper nouns should be capitalized (unless using a colon, period, question mark, or exclamation point; then the first letter after the punctuation should also be capitalized)

> *Living with my mother*

- A television broadcast should list the city, state, and the name of the studio

> Detroit, MI: WNET

Television Series

- In general, a television series should list the producer, date, title [Television series], city, state, and station

> Jackson, L. (Producer). (2001, July 17). *The human body* [Television series]. New York: WMEP.

- In general, a specific television episode from a television series should list the writer(s) and director(s), publication date, episode title [Television series episode], series producer, series title, city, state, and station

> Cantrell, C. (Writer), & Donato, C. (Director). (1979). Swimming with the big fish [Television series episode]. In T. Jones (Producer), *San Francisco Bay*. Los Angeles: WMEW.

Television series

- A television episode title from a television series should not be italicized or placed in quotation marks, only the first letter and proper nouns should be capitalized (unless using a colon, period, question mark, or exclamation point; then the first letter after the punctuation should also be capitalized)

> The night we found each other

- A television series should be italicized, and only the first letter and proper nouns should be capitalized (unless using a colon, period, question mark, or exclamation point;

then the first letter after the punctuation should also be capitalized)

> *One big happy family*

- A television series should list the city, state, and name of the studio

> Detroit, MI: WNET

Audio Recordings

- In general, an audio recording should list the major contributors, publication date, title [medium], city, state, and distributor

> Tartanian, J. Z. (Speaker). (2002). *If U.S. companies were graded on their retention strategies, many would fail* [Cassette]. Rochester Hills, MI: Metropolitan Business Institute.

- An audio recording title should be italicized, and only the first letter and proper nouns should be capitalized (unless using a colon, period, question mark, or exclamation point; then the first letter after the punctuation should also be capitalized)

Audio recordings

> *Rediscovering love in marriage*

- An audio recording should list the city and state where the audio was made and the name of the distributor

> Los Angeles: American Relationship Institute

Music Recordings

- In general, a music recording should list the writer(s), date of copyright, song title, recording artist (if different from writer), album title [medium], city, state, label, and recording date of the version (if different from copyright date)

> Barries, D. (1956). Johnny move over [Recorded by Ted Barker]. On *Songs that rock* [CD]. Springfield, MO: Pezzy Records (1987).

- A music recording song title should not be italicized or placed in quotation marks, and only the first letter and proper nouns should be capitalized (unless using a colon, period, question mark, or exclamation point; then the first letter after the punctuation should also be capitalized)

> One step closer to God

Music recordings

- A music recording album title should be italicized, and only the first letter and proper nouns should be capitalized (unless using a colon, period, question mark, or exclamation point; then the first letter after the punctuation should also be capitalized)

> *Kiss: Live at Tiger Stadium*

- A music recording should list the city and state where the recording was made and the name of the label

> Baltimore: SMD Records

Computer Software

- Computer software should list the author(s), date, title (name), (version if provided), [program], [software], or [manual], city, state, and organization

> Parnello, J. (2004). Production output analyzer [Computer software]. Buffalo, NY: Spectra Systems.

- A software, program, or language title (name) should not be italicized or put in quotation marks, and only the first letter and proper nouns should be capitalized (unless using a colon, period, question mark, or exclamation point; then the first letter after the punctuation should also be capitalized)

> Statistical software for marketing program development

- A software, program, or language source should list the city and name of the producing organization

Computer software

> Springfield, IL: Vision Analytics

Electronic Media (Internet)

- Internet resources are often the most difficult to properly list since addresses change, move, or become unavailable
- Be certain to accurately transcribe the entire address, using upper and lowercase letters exactly as they appear (copy and paste the address if possible)

Internet

- If the document referenced has been modified (e.g., the format differs, data has been added, or no page numbers are listed), then a retrieval date should be added (if unsure about modification, list the retrieval date)
- If a URL needs to be divided between lines, attempt to do so after a slash and do not hyphenate. If the URL ends the entry, do not use a period at the end of the entry
- List page numbers if available

Internet Journals (and other periodicals)

- A journal article read on the internet that was originally in print should list the author(s), publication date, article title [Electronic version], journal title, volume, issue, and pages

> Ostroff, C. (1998). The relationship between satisfaction, attitudes, and performance: An organizational level analysis [Electronic version]. *Journal of Applied Psychology, 12*(2), 963-974.

- A journal article modified on the internet that was originally in print should list the author(s), publication date, article title, journal title, volume, issue, pages, retrieval date, and URL

> Griffeth, R.W., Hom, P. W., & Gaertner, S. (2000). A meta-analysis of antecedents and correlates of employee turnover: Update, moderator tests, and research implications for the next millennium. *Journal of Management, 26*(3), 463-476. Retrieved July 21, 2004, from http://www.nwlink.com/~donplark/leader/learnor2.html

Internet journals

- Journal titles should be italicized, using upper and lower-case letters (significant words should be capitalized)

> *Journal of Sociology*

- An article title should not be italicized or placed in quotation marks, and only the first letter and proper nouns should be capitalized (unless using a colon, period, question mark, or exclamation point; then the first letter after the punctuation should also be capitalized)

> A statistical analysis of employee turnover in retail

Other Internet Documents (non-periodicals)

- In general, if no date is provided, n.d. should be utilized
- A document with no author or date should list the title, (n.d.), retrieval date, and URL
- Internet titles should be italicized, using upper and lower-case letters (significant words should be capitalized)

> *Hispanic men in the corporate world.* (n.d.). Retrieved March 25, 2004, from http://www.psychek.com/psy/edu.htm

- A document from an organization with several URLs and no publication date should list the organization, (n.d.), title, retrieval date, and homepage URL

Healthy Living Foundation. (n.d.). *Living sugar free.* Retrieved August 22, 2004, from http://www.hlf.org

- A section or chapter from a document from an organization should list should list the organization, publication date, title, document, chapter, retrieval date, and URL

National Business Research Council. (2003). Ten commandments of negotiation. In *Standards for conducting business* (chap. 3). Retrieved March 3, 2004, from http://www.nbrc.org/standards

Internet documents

- A document obtained from a university program or department website should list the author(s), publication date, title, retrieval date, university, department (use a colon after the department name), and URL

Johns, K., & Sims P. T. (2003). *Social structures within political organizations.* Retrieved June 22, 2004, from Morton University, Institute for Sociology Web Site: http://www.mu.edu/publications/papers.html

Internet Technical Reports and Research

- A report from a university (available on a private website) should list the university or organization, publication date, title, retrieval date, and URL

University of Michigan, Ann Arbor, Institute for Chemistry Research. (2000, July). *Total quality in chemistry: A new concept.* Retrieved July 25, 2004, from World Work Web site: http://www.worldwork.stp.com/~lo/ 96.02/0123.html

- A U.S. government report on an agency web site with no publication date should list the agency, (n.d.), title, retrieval date, and URL

> Federal Bureau of Investigation. (n.d.). *Overview of white-collar crime in the United States*. Retrieved September 11, 2004, from http://www.fbi.doc.gov/bbi/trade.htm

Internet reports

- A report or research title should be italicized, and only the first letter and proper nouns should be capitalized (unless using a colon, period, question mark, or exclamation point; then the first letter after the punctuation should also be capitalized)

> *Psychology in interpersonal relationships: A qualitative analysis*

Internet Meetings and Symposia

- A paper presented at a virtual conference should list the author(s), date, title, conference, retrieval date, and URL

> Merrill, T. J. (2004). *Merrill communication climate report*. Paper presented at Merrill 2004 virtual conference. Retrieved July 29, 2004, from http://www.merrill.com/ topicofthemonth/press.html

- A paper or abstract title from a meeting or symposium should be italicized, and only the first letter and proper nouns should be capitalized (unless using a colon, period, question mark, or exclamation point; then the first letter after the punctuation should also be capitalized)

> *Psychological impact studies*

On-line Newspaper Articles from a Database

- An on-line daily newspaper article from a database should list the author(s), entire publication date, article title, newspaper title, retrieval date, and database

Hewlett, M. T. (2003, March 23). Education helps stop turnover. *Boston Herald*. Retrieved July 24, 2004, from ProQuest.

- Newspaper titles should be italicized, using upper and lowercase letters (significant words should be capitalized)

The Buffalo Tribune

- An article title should not be italicized or placed in quotation marks, and only the first letter and proper nouns should be capitalized (unless using a colon, period, question mark, or exclamation point; then the first letter after the punctuation should also be capitalized)

On-line newspaper articles

Atlanta undergoes an image change

On-line Newspaper Articles from the Internet

- An on-line daily newspaper article from the Internet should list the author(s), entire publication date, article title, newspaper title, retrieval date, and URL

Hewlett, M. T. (2003, March 23). Education helps stop turnover. *Boston Herald*. Retrieved July 24, 2004, from http://www.bostonherald.com

- Newspaper titles should be italicized, using upper and lowercase letters (significant words should be capitalized)

Internet newspaper articles

The Seattle Times

- An article title should not be italicized or placed in quotation marks, and only the first letter and proper nouns should be capitalized (unless using a colon, period, question mark, or exclamation point; then the first letter after the punctuation should also be capitalized)

> Urban sprawl affects classroom space

On-line Magazine/Journal Articles from a Database

- An on-line magazine or journal article from a database should list the author(s), publication date, article title, magazine/journal title, volume, issue, pages, retrieval date, and database

> Henning, P., & Stein, J. (2003). A controlled study of aggression: Inside a federal prison. *Journal of Experimental Psychology, 41*(2), 102-116. Retrieved March 23, 2004, from InfoTrac (Expanded Academic).

On-line magazine/ journal articles

- Magazine and journal titles should be italicized, using upper and lowercase letters (significant words should be capitalized)

> *Journal of Social Psychology*

- An article title should not be italicized or placed in quotation marks, and only the first letter and proper nouns should be capitalized (unless using a colon, period, question mark, or exclamation point; then the first letter after the punctuation should also be capitalized)

> An analysis of workplace behavior in non-profit organizations

On-line Magazine/Journal Articles from the Internet

- An on-line magazine or journal article retrieved from the Internet should list the author(s), publication date, article title, journal title, volume, issue, pages, retrieval date, and URL

> Henning, P., & Stein, J. (2003). A controlled study of aggression: Inside a federal prison. *Journal of Experimental Psychology, 41*(2), 102-116. Retrieved March 23, 2004, from http://www.expsych.com

- Magazine and journal titles should be italicized, using upper and lowercase letters (significant words should be capitalized)

> *Journal of Organizational Studies*

- An article title should not be italicized or placed in quotation marks, and only the first letter and proper nouns should be capitalized (unless using a colon, period, question mark, or exclamation point; then the first letter after the punctuation should also be capitalized)

> An analysis of workplace behavior in non-profit organizations

Internet
magazine/
journal
articles

On-line U.S. Government Reports from GPO Access Databases

- An on-line U.S. government report from a GPO Access database should list the agency, publication date, title, retrieval date, and database

On-line reports

> U.S. Council on Aging. (2003, June). *Aging baby boomers: Are we ready for their retirement?* Retrieved November 23, 2003, from http://www.access.gpo.gov/aging/index.html

- A report title should be italicized, and only the first letter and proper nouns should be capitalized (unless using a colon, period, question mark, or exclamation point; then the first letter after the punctuation should also be capitalized)

> *Government bonds: Investing with confidence*

Part Three

Sample Paper

The following excerpts from the book *Modern Day CEOs* by Michael F. Heberling and Peggy M. Houghton were reprinted with permission from the authors. Some changes have been made to the original document to adhere to the APA standards described in this handbook. Because only portions of the text have been retrieved, the reading is not verbatim from the actual book.

The page header begins on the title page and is placed on all subsequent pages. Use the first two or three words of the title, five spaces, and the appropriate page number.

Running head: OPRAH WINFREY

Note that the h in Running head is lowercase. Also, the actual title appears in all caps. Finally, after Running head: a total of 50 characters (including spaces) can be used. Therefore, if the title is less than a total of 50 characters, the entire title is provided. Otherwise, only the major words are included.

Title of Paper

Student Name

Name of College or University

Title of the paper

Name of student

Name of college or university

Abstract

Oprah Winfrey is a world-renowned figure… basically a household name. The accomplishments earned throughout her lifetime are nothing less than stellar. Her die-hard followers and fans simply consider her a friend, someone they can relate with. They consider her to be a caring, loving, and compassionate individual. She had the conviction, desire, and ambition to overcome both childhood and professional obstacles that most would consider insurmountable. The chances of her succeeding in life were slim, to say the least. She not only beat the odds, she climbed to the top. Her celebrity status never reached her ego; and, to date, Oprah Winfrey is one of the most successful female entertainers/entrepreneurs in the world.

The word Abstract is centered on the page. The abstract Is the only part of an APA document where the first paragraph is *not* indented. The abstract should be only one paragraph in length and not exceed 120 words.

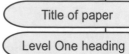

Title of paper ──── Oprah Winfrey

Level One heading ──── Oprah...the Early Days

Oprah Gail Winfrey was born January 29, 1954. Her name was actually Orpah, a name that came from the Bible's book of Ruth. Although her birth certificate reads Orpah, most people did not know how to pronounce it. People generally reversed two of the letters, thus creating the name *Oprah* (Brands, 1999).

Oprah's mother had multiple relationships throughout her lifetime. During some of these relationships, she would ask to have Oprah return to live with her. Although she preferred not to reside with her mother, she was forced to acquiesce. Yet, each time, Oprah never stayed for a long period of time. During one of her extended stays with her mother, Oprah's life would be scarred forever. When her mother left for work, Oprah was often left with an older male cousin. She always felt very uncomfortable being in the young man's presence. It was during one of these days, that her cousin would rape her. Oprah was told by the cousin never to say a word; if she were to say something, both of them would be in terrible trouble. Oprah agreed never to divulge anything. Unfortunately, this was not the only rape that would occur. Oprah was repeatedly raped in her own home by people who would visit her family. These terrible crimes resulted in Oprah possessing horribly low self-esteem...something that has had a deep effect on her till this day (Brands, 1999).

Brands further noted that throughout her troubled youth, Oprah would always have a refuge. She would turn to books as a safe haven. She was, and still is, an avid reader. Reading gave her hope and gave her the will to aspire to new goals. Oprah was exceptionally intelligent. Her strong intellect allowed her to skip both kindergarten and second grade. Oprah always praised her teachers for their guidance and support throughout her early years (1999).

Although Oprah lived with a myriad of people throughout her lifetime, she credits her grandmother for making her the success that she is today. This is primarily because her grandmother acted as the dominant support figure during her youth. It was her grandmother, and later her father, who were the ones who expected the best out of her; they expected her to excel with everything she attempted. Time would prove this to be an expectation that was ultimately conquered (Brands, 1999).

Adolescent Problems

Oprah's academic success was not enough to prevent personal struggles. She was continually ridiculed for being an African American. In an effort to gain attention and affection, she became sexually active. This ultimately resulted in a teenage pregnancy; the baby was born prematurely and died shortly thereafter. Oprah would eventually end up moving back with her father and stepmother. These two individuals were strict and wanted desperately for Oprah to change her lifestyle. They expected Oprah to study endlessly and allowed her to watch

> Paraphrased example with the author's name appearing at the beginning of the paragraph, and the year published noted at the end of the paragraph. The punctuation (period) is placed after the actual year.

> Level Three heading

television for only one hour a day...the local and national news (Raatma, 2001).

During her sophomore year at college, she was encouraged to apply for a position at WTVF, a CBS television station in Nashville. When it came time to audition, her strategy was to imitate her idol, Barbara Walters. The technique was a success, and she was offered the job (Raatma, 2001).

While in her senior year in college, Raatma (2001) noted that another position became available to Oprah. This job, a reporter and co-anchor for the evening news, would require her to move to Baltimore, Maryland. She decided to take the venture. Her father was disappointed that she did not complete college, but she vowed that she would be back to finalize her studies.

She had mixed reviews in her new position. Some people felt that she was too emotional for the job. Her critics said that she would sometimes mispronounce words because she preferred to report impromptu as opposed to following a script. Since the station had signed a long-term contract with Oprah, they felt that they would find a new position for her. In 1977, a new station manager approached Oprah with yet another proposition. He decided to start a talk show titled *People are Talking*. This program would resemble the then most prominent television talk show available...*Phil Donahue*. The format of the program would allow members of the audience to participate in the show. It would be hosted by two individuals...a male and female (Brands, 1999).

Example of a sentence with the author near the beginning and the year published following.

Italicize the title of television shows

People are Talking would eventually beat Donahue in the Baltimore television ratings. The show was soon picked up in other cities across the United States. Oprah was becoming a well-known television personality.

Problems Associated with Success

(Level One heading)

Oprah was becoming a true icon of success professionally, but her personal life suffered. She had serious problems with relationships that evolved throughout the years. Her self-esteem was exceptionally low. When she developed a seemingly strong relationship with a member of the opposite sex, she felt obsessed with being with the person at all times. Her insecurity and lack of self-confidence clearly was due to her childhood experiences. Gayle King, her best friend and now editor of *O, The Oprah Magazine*, was always by her side offering words of encouragement. To this day, they still remain the best of friends.

(Italicize the title of a periodical)

A.M. Chicago

(Level Three heading)

Oprah's newfound success was now receiving national recognition, and she was ready for a change. About that time, the general manager of *A.M. Chicago* had viewed one of Oprah's talk show tapes. He was nothing more than stunned with her abilities. Before long, Oprah was hired to be the new host of *A.M. Chicago*. Oprah's biggest challenge was the fact that *Donahue* was based in Chicago. Many critics wondered if Oprah could compete with Donahue. Encouraged to leave Baltimore by Gayle King, Oprah took the plunge. The Chicago audience took an immediate liking to Oprah. So much so, that she eventually beat *Donahue* in ratings (Brands, 1999).

Within 12 weeks, *A. M. Chicago* had more viewers than *Donahue*. Seven months later, her show was extended to one hour. She interviewed well-known celebrities such as Tom Selleck; Sally Field; Paul McCartney; and her personal idol, Barbara Walters (Brands, 1999).

The producer of the show, Debbie DiMaio, explained Oprah's secret of success in the following manner:

> She's 100% percent the same off-camera as on. People like her because they can relate to her. She's got all the same problems – overweight, boyfriend troubles, she's been poor. So when people see her on television the can say, "That's my friend Oprah." (Raatma, 2001, p. 51)

40+ word direct quote. Citation follows indented block quote; end punctuation (period) appears **before** the citation.

Her forte, however, was interviewing the "average" person. She would get ordinary people to divulge their personal traumatic experiences. These conversations were almost therapeutic to Winfrey. In fact, it was during one of her ordinary interviews that she openly discussed her most horrifying personal experience…being molested by numerous relatives and friends. According to Brands, she said

> I think it was on that day that, for the first time, I recognized that I was not to blame… It happened on the air, as so many things happen for me. It happened on the air in the middle of someone else's experience, and I thought I was going to have a breakdown on television. (1999, p. 298)

40+ word direct quote. Author's name appears at the beginning of the quote; year and page number are at the end. Again, because the quote is 40+ words, the punctuation (period) is placed **before** the citation.

The Food Battle

Fear of failure was Oprah's greatest downfall. One way in which to deal with her mounting stress was food. Eating gave her comfort. Unfortunately, it also caused her to gain a great deal of weight... something she still has difficulty controlling. Her eating habits soon became out of control. Oprah would binge diet and lose substantial weight. She would meet regularly with nutritionists and dieticians. This would work temporarily; but as soon as the pressure began to mount again, the eating would start as well (Lowe, 1998).

Due to a lawsuit hearing, Oprah was forced to tape her show from Texas for a period of time. Oprah spent many hours defending her actions in the courtroom. During her stay, she actually gained 11 pounds. She noted, "I was strategizing with lawyers at night. I couldn't help but eat pie" (Lowe, 1998, p. 111).

Oprah's Empire

The Oprah Winfrey Show

Oprah Winfrey soon gained the reputation (and ratings) of being number one in the talk show business. She was able to sympathize and, quite literally, *empathize* with others in desperate need. She suggested solutions to the various problems her shows revealed. She would recommend books for her guests and audiences to read. These books would soon become best sellers. Consequently, the publishing companies suddenly became knocking on her door. They deluged her with books to read; review; and, most importantly, potentially endorse on her television program.

> Less than 40 word direct quote in quotation marks. End punctuation (period) appears *after* the citation.

> Level One heading

The Classroom

Having the urge to test her skills at teaching, Oprah and her fiancé, Stedman Graham, agreed to team-teach a course at the Northwestern University. Bill Dedman writes in his article titled *Professor Oprah: Preaching what she practices* that Oprah described her success as coming from setting goals and from achieving them. She described the value of having an authentic leadership style that matched one's personality. Leaders must look inward, admit mistakes, and recognize their weaknesses (1999).

O, The Oprah Magazine

In 2000, Oprah attempted to conquer yet another goal. She took on the position as magazine founder and editorial director of *O, The Oprah Magazine*. The magazine is published monthly and encourages readers to make the most out of life. It offers celebrity interviews, articles about health and nutrition, self-help columns, and much more (Raatma, 2001).

As noted in Raatma (2001), Oprah described the magazine's purpose in the following manner:

My hope is that this magazine will help you lead a more productive life, one in which you feel a sense of vitality, cooperation, harmony, balance and reverence within yourself and in your encounters. That doesn't mean living a life without frustration, anxieties and disappointments. It means understanding that your choices move you forward or hold you back. (p. 93)

After the first issue was ripped off the stands, Oprah still was not content with the magazine.

The author's name appears at the beginning of the paragraph, and the year is at the end to tie it together. This provides for a varied writing style.

Clemetson writes in her *Newsweek* article (2001) that Winfrey complained that the layouts were not lush enough and that the writing was not smart enough. She ordered several re-shoots and revisions for the second edition. By the third issue, the editor in chief resigned. Oprah was able to secure a new editor who, like herself, is a perfectionist.

A Day with Oprah

Oprah Winfrey is a dedicated, die-hard professional. She is a perfectionist who expects the same from her staff. People who worked for Oprah do so with extreme loyalty. They work long hours and put forth great sacrifice to keep up with Oprah's demands. One former producer noted the following, "People adore her. They give up their lives for her. People who work [at Harpo] get divorced, put off having kids, have no outside lives. Because everything, all your time and energy, is given to Oprah" (as cited in Raatma, 2001, p. 80).

Example of a secondary source citation.

Oprah is used to total control. She is a shrewd businesswoman, who signs all checks in excess of $1,000 for her Harpo Entertainment Group. She has also been known to scrutinize the smaller checks that others on her staff have the authority to sign for. She attempts to bind all employees to strict, lifelong confidentiality agreements. She keeps a keen eye on her personal ventures as well. In the past, she barred the press from the course she taught with Stedman Graham at Northwestern University's business school. Students who chose to talk to reporters could face disciplinary action from the school (Clemetson, 2001).

Example of a paragraph ending with author, date reference citation.

Down-to-earth diva... control freak... silly... caring... perfectionist... optimist. These are all words that accurately describe Oprah Winfrey. Clemetson (2001) describes a typical day with Oprah:

> It's Friday afternoon, and Oprah Winfrey is in an otherworldly state of calm. Her staff, however, is frantic. Nelson Mandela is about to arrive for a TV interview, and producers are rushing through set-checks, tightening security and prepping audience members. Behind the closed double doors to her Chicago office, Winfrey is plopped down in a cushiony armchair, a candle burning at her side, talking about the past year, when as assistant calls in a panic. Mr. Mandela is 30 minutes early, and Winfrey is still in her off-air gear–a baggy sweater and a well-worn pair of pants. "He'll just have to see me with no makeup on," says Winfrey, raking a hand through her unstyled hair. At least a little foundation and powder? The caller pleads. "Look," Winfrey replies before hanging up the phone, "he's seen a woman with no makeup on before." Her instincts are right. Mandela is charmed by the casual welcome.
>
> Four days later, Winfrey is in perfectionist mode. Looking back at the December issue of her new magazine, *O*, she holds up the cover and winces. "Ooh, there's a mistake!" she says, pointing to the word "generosity," which she thinks should have bigger type. Annoyed with herself for not spotting it sooner, she grabs a stack of past issues and

Second (and subsequent) paragraph in a block direct quote is indented

starts flipping. "Didn't like that." Flip. "Nope. Never got that right." Flip. Flip. Realizing that she's obsessing, she blows out a whoosh of breath and refocuses her energy on pages she likes. After several satisfied nods, she returns to the December issue and declares: "I love everything in this!" Then she turns a page, spots another imperceptible glitch and adds sheepishly: "Except this. We should have moved this." (pp. 43-44)

> Use the abbreviation pp. when referring to more than one page

It is clear that, as Winfrey's assets continue to grow at exponential rates, micromanaging will not be a feasible option for the multimillionaire. She will simply have to give up some amount of control in some areas. She will probably do this very grudgingly – but there will be no alternative.

Oprah's Ten Commandments

Millions of words have been written about Oprah and her many temperaments. Writers have dissected her as an actress, an entertainer, a counselor, a business leader, and as a female success in a male-dominated world. But in order to really delve into her complex persona, it is important to find out what she thinks of herself, and what she views as her outlook on her success. Readers can gain some extremely valuable insight into her inner feelings from a set of 10 commandments that she says guide her success (Lowe, 1998, pp. 168-169). They include the following:

1. Don't live your life to please others.
2. Don't depend on forces outside of yourself to get ahead.

3. Seek harmony and compassion in your business and personal life.
4. Get rid of the back-stabbers—surround yourself only with people who will lift you higher.
5. Be nice.
6. Rid yourself of your addictions—whether they be food, alcohol, drugs, or behavior habits.
7. Surround yourself with people who are as smart or smarter than yourself.
8. If money is your motivation, forget it.
9. Never hand over your power to someone else.
10. Be persistent in pursuing your dreams.

Conclusion

Winfrey is a tireless businesswoman with endless energy. She is constantly working to accomplish her goals. She is a philanthropist who has donated millions to various charities. She is also an actress, television producer, CEO, and educator with a personal fortune estimated in excess of $800 million. She is obviously a very talented, very busy, very complex person. There is no question about the fact that she is a leader – but the thing she is most proud of is the fact that the American people relate to her and consider her their good friend.

References

Brands, H.W. (1999). *Masters of enterprise.* New York: Simon & Schuster, Inc.

Branham, C. (1998). *Profiles of great African Americans.* Lincolnwood, IL: Publications Interna- tional, Ltd.

Clemetson, L. (2001, January 8). Oprah on Oprah. *Newsweek, 137,* 38-44+. Retrieved November 23, 2004, from ProQuest.

Dedman, B. (1999, October 10). Professor Oprah, preaching what she practices. *New York Times,* p. C1..

Landrum, G. (1997). *Profiles of Black success.* Amherst, NY: Prometheus Books.

Lowe, J. (1998) *Oprah Winfrey speaks: Insight from the world's most influential voice.* New York: John Wiley & Sons, Inc.

Raatma, L. (2001). *Oprah Winfrey entertainer, producer, and businesswoman.* Chicago: Ferguson Publishing Company.

The word References Is centered on the page; no colon is necessary

Example of a book entry

Example of an article retrieved from an on-line database

Index

In-Text Entries and Formatting

Reference Page Entries